BO
W

TO: Kathy

FROM: Love, Pat

Happy Birthday

2017!

OMMM

ARF

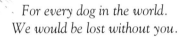

For every dog in the world.
We would be lost without you.

Designed by Kathy Weller

Text and illustrations copyright © 2015 Kathy Weller
Published by Peter Pauper Press, Inc.
202 Mamaroneck Avenue
White Plains, NY 10601
ISBN 978-1-4413-1750-6
Printed in China
7 6 5 4 3 2 1

Visit us at www.peterpauper.com

HAVE YOU EVER WONDERED
WHAT YOUR DOG IS THINKING?

THE
ANCIENT AND ARCANE
TRUTHS
OF THE
INNER WORLD
OF
DOMESTIC CANINES
ARE NOW
FINALLY EXPLAINED
WITH
DOGGY YOGA

...WHY DOES HE DO THE THINGS HE DOES?

MEDITATE ON THE AGE-OLD WISDOM INHERENT IN EACH DOGGY YOGA POSE, AND ENJOY A DEEPER UNDERSTANDING OF YOUR FURRY FRIEND THAN EVER BEFORE.

NAMASTE.

FOUNDATION POSES

MOUNTAIN POSE

MOUNTAIN POSE IS
A STARTING POINT
FOR MANY OF THE
DOGGY YOGA POSTURES.

BE SEATED COMFORTABLY
ON GROUND. EYES BRIGHT
AND ALERT, YET RELAXED.

STRONG AND STILL,
STABLE AND ENDURING,
MOUNTAIN POSE EMBODIES
THESE WONDERFUL QUALITIES
OF MAN'S BEST FRIEND,
AND MORE.

NAMASTE.

SPHINX POSE

BEGIN IN MOUNTAIN POSE.
RETIRE TO FLOOR.
CROUCH ON ALL FOURS.

• • •

THIS IS AN UPRIGHT STANCE,
ACTIVE BUT RELAXED.
PAWS STRAIGHT OUT IN
FRONT, REAR LEGS BEHIND
AND TUCKED IN.

• • •

EMBODY AND EMBRACE
YOUR KARMIC REGALITY
IN THIS POSE.

• • •

BREATHE DEEPLY
AND RHYTHMICALLY.

CORPSE POSE

BEGIN IN SPHINX POSE.

• • •

ROLL ONTO BACK AND EMBRACE
A COMPLETE RELEASE
OF DOGGY TENSION.

• • •

JUST RELAX INTO THE POSE.

• • •

MEDITATE.

{ SNORE-CHANTING ENCOURAGED. }

PROP: HUMAN

STANDING SPLIT POSE

SIDE PLANK POSE

BEGIN IN CORPSE POSE.
ROLL MINDFULLY ONTO SIDE.

• • •

REACH PAWS OUT LONG
IN FRONT OF YOU.

• • •

REACH BACK LEGS
FAR BEHIND YOU.

• • •

STRETCH DEEPLY AND
BREATHE THROUGH CHAKRAS,
FROM TAIL TO NOSE AND BACK.

• • •

BODY SHOULD FORM ONE
LONG, ORGANIC LINE.

• • •

STAY IN THIS POSE
INDEFINITELY.

NAMASTE.

ACTIVE POSES

GATE POSE

PROPS: KITTY, COUCH

THE OBJECT OF GATE POSE
IS TO GAIN PEACE OF MIND
BY PROTECTING A SPACE
FROM UNDESIRABLE
KITTY KARMA.

BEGIN IN MOUNTAIN POSE
AT FRONT OF COUCH.
SIT STRONG AND STEADY.

• • •

WITH CLEAR INTENTION,
FOCUS ON PROTECTING
COUCH FROM KITTY CHAKRA.
USE STRENGTH AND
FLEXIBILITY MOVEMENTS
WHEN NEEDED.

• • •

CONTINUE MOVEMENTS
UNTIL KITTY CHAKRA
RELOCATES TO OTHER ROOM.

SIDE-RECLINING LEG LIFT POSE

FIG. 1

BEGIN IN MOUNTAIN OR SPHINX POSE.

LIFT AND LOWER BACK LEG IN A CIRCULAR MOTION, USING THE PAW TO GENTLY BUT ENERGETICALLY MASSAGE SIDE OF BODY.

FOR SYMMETRY AND BALANCE, REPEAT ON OTHER SIDE. YOGI MAY REPEAT ENTIRE SEQUENCE AS OFTEN AS DESIRED.

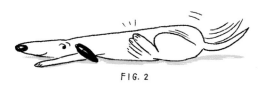

FIG. 2

FROM MOUNTAIN POSE (FIG.1)
THIS IS AN ACTIVE BUT RELAXED POSE IN AN UPRIGHT STANCE.

FROM SPHINX POSE (FIG.2)
THIS IS A MORE PASSIVE SEQUENCE, PERFORMED ON ALL FOURS.

WHEEL POSE

STAND ON ALL FOURS. ACTIVATE YOUR TAIL'S ENERGY CHAKRA.

• • •

FOLLOW IT IN A CIRCULAR MOTION, SLOWLY AND STEADILY AT FIRST, THEN BUILDING UP SPEED AND INTENSITY IN A CIRCULAR DANCE OF CELEBRATION AND RELEASE.

• • •

END SEQUENCE ON FLOOR IN CORPSE POSE.

UPWARD DOG POSE

PROPS: TABLE, TREATS

BEGIN IN MOUNTAIN POSE
NEAR HIGH TABLE UPON
WHICH RESTS A TASTY NUGGET
OF APPETITE ENERGY.

· · ·

USING STRONG BACK LEGS,
HOP UP, REACHING TABLE EDGE
WITH STABLE STRENGTH.
STRETCH NECK LONG AND
USE NOSE TO REACH UP
TO TOUCH APPETITE ENERGY.

· · ·

CONTINUE TO SPIRIT ENERGY
TO EDGE OF TABLE UNTIL IT
FINALLY DANCES TO THE GROUND.

· · ·

END POSE WITH
INGESTION CEREMONY.

· · ·

SANTOSHA.

TRIANGLE POSE

PROP: LEASH

STAND ON ALL FOURS
BY FRONT DOOR.
CROSS REAR LEGS TIGHTLY,
CREATING A
TRIANGLE FORMATION.

• • •

THIS WILL CLEARLY INDICATE
TO NEARBY HUMAN THAT
THE VINYASA FLOW OF
THE PEE CHAKRA
NEEDS KARMIC RELEASE.

• • •

THIS POSE WILL ALSO
PROVIDE A TEMPORARY
PHYSIOLOGICAL STABILIZATION
OF THE PEE CHAKRA.

HANDSTAND POSE

PROP: LOW STOOL

BEGIN POSE SEATED ON LOW
STOOL OR HIGH CUSHION.

• • •

BEGIN DISMOUNTING FROM SEATING
PROP BY PLACING FRONT PAWS
ON GROUND IN FRONT OF YOU,
ONE AT A TIME.

• • •

WITH TRUNK AND HINDQUARTERS
STILL SUPPORTED ON SEAT,
REMAIN IN THIS POSITION,
STEADY AND BALANCED.

• • •

CONTINUE THIS RELAXED
POSE INDEFINITELY.

TIP: HUMANS FIND THIS POSE
ENTERTAINING. USE THIS TO
YOUR KARMIC ADVANTAGE.

PROP: HUMAN

UPWARD SALUTE POSE

SIT ON HINDQUARTERS,
SPINE STRAIGHT,
GAZE ALERT,
WITH AN ENERGIZED
AND PEACEFUL MIND.

• • •

AS HUMAN REACHES
OUT TO YOU,
PLACE YOUR PAW IN HAND.

SMILE AND WAG TAIL.
BE HAPPY. FEEL LOVED.

CAT POSE

PROP:CAT

BEGIN IN SIDE PLANK POSE
BEHIND CAT CHAKRA.

INHALE AND EXHALE.

WITH BOTH PAWS, REACH
FAR IN FRONT OF YOU
FOR CAT'S TAIL.

(DO NOT YET TOUCH TAIL.)

WITH ONE ENERGETIC
LUNGE, CAPTURE THE TAIL,
SURPRISING CAT CHAKRA.

FEEL THE ENERGY FLY
IN A MOMENT OF
KARMIC ELEVATION.

OUTDOOR
POSES

DEAD BUG POSE

BEGIN POSE IN NATURE SETTING.

• • •

CLOSE EYES AND MEDITATE TO LISTEN
FOR BUZZING VIBRATION OF BUG CHAKRA.

• • •

ONCE DETECTED, ROLL WITH ACTIVE
ENERGY TO CAREFULLY CAPTURE BUG
CHAKRA. ENJOY THE SPIRITED DANCE
OF THE CHAKRA ENERGY.

• • •

RELEASE AND RECAPTURE
TO REPEAT SEQUENCE.

{ NO BUG CHAKRA WAS HARMED
IN THE MAKING OF THIS BOOK. }

PROP: BUG

HALF MOON POSE

PERFORM THIS POSE
AT NIGHT DURING HALF MOON
FOR MOST SYNERGIZED
AND SPIRITUAL PRACTICE.

• • •

BEGIN IN MOUNTAIN POSE,
NOSE TO NIGHT SKY.

• • •

INHALE DEEPLY,
THEN VOCALIZE PRIMAL ENERGY
TOWARD MOON CHAKRA.

• • •

REPEAT SEQUENCE.

• • •

END POSE WHEN HUMAN
SPIRITS YOU INDOORS.

PIGEON POSE

BEGIN IN MOUNTAIN POSE
UNDER ROOST OF
PIGEON CHAKRAS.

CENTER CHI.
INHALE.
EXHALE.

PUSH OFF HIND LEGS, REACH
UP GATE, AND STRETCH.
BEGIN DIRECTING ENERGY
CHANT TOWARD PIGEON CHAKRAS.

REPEAT SEQUENCE UNTIL
PIGEON CHAKRAS ARE
FULLY ENERGIZED.

NAMASTE.

PROPS: PIGEONS, GATE

PLOW POSE

PROP: BONE "GIFT"

OUTDOORS,
ACTIVATE SENSITIVE
SNIFFING PRANA
TO LOCATE AREA
OF BURIED GIFT.

• • •

APPROACH AREA WITH
QUIET MOVEMENTS.
WHEN DIRECTLY ABOVE
THE SPOT OF BURIAL,
ENGAGE PLOW POSE BY
DIGGING FOR GIFT
UNTIL IT IS UNVEILED.

• • •

ONCE FOUND,
ENJOY CHEWING
ON DELICIOUS GIFT.

AFTER,
MEDITATE ON GRATITUDE.

MULTI-POSE SEQUENCES

EAGLE POSE

PROP: SQUIRREL

START IN MOUNTAIN POSE.

FOLLOW BREATH TO
ALLOW BODY TO GO EASY.

• • •

DROP LEGS AND LET THEM
STRETCH OUT IN WIDE
RESTORATIVE POSE.

• • •

RELAX BACK.

• • •

HOLD POSE INDEFINITELY.

NOTE: THIS POSE IS AN
EFFECTIVE WAY TO ENTERTAIN
THE HUMANS EFFORTLESSLY.

MEDITATION POSES

PROP: WATER

PEACOCK POSE

STAND STRONG ON ALL
FOURS, ON SOLID GROUND.

• • •

ALLOW FRESH WATER TO
RINSE YOUR FUR CHAKRA
AND CLEANSE AWAY
ALL SOILED ENERGY.

• • •

AT CULMINATION OF SEQUENCE,
SPIRIT THE FUR CHAKRA
INTO AN ACTIVE, SHIMMERING
CIRCLE OF POSITIVE ENERGY,
LIKE THE BEAUTIFUL
FEATHERS OF A PEACOCK.

THIS MEDITATIVE POSE
REQUIRES A STILL BODY
AND A QUIET MIND.

IN BASIN CONTAINING
SHALLOW WATER,
SIT IN MOUNTAIN POSE.

• • •

EMBRACE YOUR INNER ZEN
AS HUMAN HANDS
LATHER AND SCRUB
YOUR FUR CHAKRA CLEAN.

• • •

PRACTICE DHARMA OF STILLNESS
THROUGHOUT SEQUENCE, THEN
FOLLOW WITH PEACOCK POSE.

FULL BOAT POSE

PROP: BASIN OF WATER

SIT TALL IN MOUNTAIN
POSE AT BASE OF TREE.

• • •

RAISE HEAD UP TO SKY
TO LOCATE SQUIRREL
CHAKRA VIBRATION.

• • •

WHEN VISIBLE, JUMP UP ON
HIND LEGS, STRETCHING
TALL AGAINST BASE OF TREE
AND DIRECT A HARMONIC
CHANT TOWARD SQUIRREL.

THIS WILL FILL LITTLE
SQUIRREL WITH SPIRITED,
ANIMATED ENERGY.